I MOVED ALL MY
WOMEN UPSTAIRS

NEWFOUNDLAND POETRY SERIES

The Newfoundland Poetry Series was started in 1993 as
Breakwater's twentieth anniversary project to honour and
preserve the literary talents of our Newfoundland and Labrador
poets. Our aim is to make the series affordable to as many
lovers of poetry as possible.

Books currently available in the series:

> *bending with the wind*, nick avis
>
> *Allowing the Light*, Mary Dalton
>
> *Talking to Ghosts*, Philip Gardner
>
> *Dancing in Limbo*, Al Pittman
>
> *Landscapes of Time*, Alastair Macdonald
>
> *Timely Departures*, Randall Maggs
>
> *Voices of the Young*, various contributors
>
> *Republic of Solitude*, Richard Green
>
> *And You, Blessed Healer*, Boyd Chubbs
>
> *I Moved All My Women Upsairs*, Roberta Buchanan
>
> *now the moon appears among the lilies*,
> Susan Ingersoll

I MOVED ALL MY WOMEN UPSTAIRS

ROBERTA BUCHANAN

BREAKWATER

BREAKWATER
100 Water Street
P.O. Box 2188
St. John's, NF
A1C 6E6

The Publisher acknowledges the financial assistance of the Canada Council in anticipation of a block grant for 1998.

The author gratefully acknowledges the financial assistance of the Newfoundland and Labrador Arts Council.

Cover image: John Andrews
Author photo: Winifred Mellor

Canadian Cataloguing in Publication Data

Buchanan, Roberta

I moved all my women upstairs

(Newfoundland poetry series)
Poems.
ISBN: 978-1-55081-120-9

I. Title. II. Series.

PS8553.U4336I46 1997   C811'.54   C98-950012-8
PR9199.3.B82I46 1997
Reprinted in 1999

DEDICATION

To "Older Sister"
Lillian Bouzane

and

IN MEMORIAM

Isobel Brown

CONTENTS

I. THE WORLD ABOVE//THE WORLD BELOW

II. SEASONS

III. I MOVED ALL MY WOMEN UPSTAIRS

I. THE WORLD ABOVE//THE WORLD BELOW

THE WORLD ABOVE//THE WORLD BELOW

Down below there is a spirit
   the underwater panther
In the sky above is the thunderbird
     the world above
     and the world below
If I align myself exactly on the well
   connecting the three worlds
I can descend to the underwater panther
or fly up to the eagle spirit
The hole to the underworld is recognized by
     a square within a square

□

Everything is connected
I wear your symbols on my clothes
Panther and eagle empower me

I visit the spirits in dreams
When I wake I draw the images
on my tent, embroider them on my cloak
Their power surrounds me

   x + +

Dream of the black dog:
I embroider it on the back of my jacket
It leaps up, tongue of flame above its head
From the left steps lead downwards
Showing me the way to the underworld

10

NORN

I AM the scold   the skald
servant of the Norn
skuld   skadi
I AM the weird   the word
The weird sisters urge me
Die Schreiberinnen—women who write
the Wurd of creation
Skadi, Queen of Shades
gives me a gift
a blank sheet of paper
       face changing
       beautiful maiden, blonde braid
       old hag, black hole for face
       corpse, night-mare
I kneel and kiss her hands, her feet
She bends over me   embraces me
Her grey veils flutter in the breeze
"This is truth" she says
"both beautiful and ugly
write it on your paper
come back tomorrow
and read what you have written"

KALI POEMS

I

When I stamp my foot, watch out!
I'm losing my temper
When I dance in a rage
The whole earth shakes for fear
I AM Kali the Destroyer
SHE I AM you fear and desire
My necklace is made of the penises of my lovers
Cut off in their prime
I AM Shakti, Power
I AM the Black Goddess, Lady of the Dead
White, red and black are my colours
My menses are the Ocean of Blood
They call me DEVA, the Great Goddess
I created the magic letters of the alphabet
With which you write my name.

O the joy of stamping on the faces
Of you who have insulted me
Ignored my power, denied my existence
Relegated me to the realm of "superstition"
The joy of twisting your guts in my hands
And seeing you squirm
I AM WARNING YOU:
There was a man who sneered at me
He fell off a mountain
Broke his sacrilegious neck.

KALI POEM 2: ATTACK/C(O)UNTERATTACK

The pale young man
stands at my door
wringing wet
"Can I use your phone?"
"Of course," I say
and let him in.
He threatens me with a knife
"Get into the bedroom
Take off your clothes"
Lines carefully rehearsed
Taken from some show.
"This isn't a very nice thing
to do," I say
never having learned the part
unprepared.

I beat his face to a pulp
with a reading-lamp
shouting "I AM KALI THE DESTROYER!"
When he is limp
I jump on his corpse
My hands and face are
smeared with blood
"I AM KALI," I shout
"YOU CAN'T FUCK AROUND WITH ME."
The young man sits up
"That wasn't a very nice thing to do,"
says he.

KALI POEM 3

I wish I could grow up to be a hag
I would dance on your grave
Shouting "I am alive and you are dead!"
The oppressor downpressed at last.

I wish I could grow up to be a crone
An old wise-woman to whom the young would turn
I would give them advice all right. Like:
Kill the kill-joy in yourself. Dance and sing.
Wear the pink triangle over your genitals.
Worship the Goddess, She will provide.
Make a racket with your cymbals
Drums rattles and marimbas
Blow your own trumpet, sing your own song
Stop being quiet, silence is not golden
Don't shut up, open up.

THE PATRIARCHY RIDES ON MY BACK

The patriarchy rides on my back
Like the Old Man in Sindbad's tale
"Where's my dinner?" he shouts in my ear
His hands throttle my throat so I cannot speak
Cannot sing as I wash his dishes
Do the vacuuming.
He craps down my back and I clean it up
(Of course)
He hisses in my ear
"Women can't write. There are no women artists
Composers, conductors
Shakespeare was a MAN
So was Tchaikovsky, Wagner, Beethoven, Bach,
Picasso, Rembrandt, Degas, Gaugin, Michelangelo."
I try to hum to myself, drown out his noise
I try to distract him by pointing to the flowers
Nothing pleases him. I am too slow
Too fat, not "feminine" enough
To suit his taste (as if I wanted to)
I bear this white-man burden on my back
I am doubled over by this heavy load
I pray for his death
To be able to stand up straight, tall
To be free again.

HUSBAND

Inexorable ticking of the clock
Her heart sinks as his key grates in the lock;
He's home from work
Sullen dinner, empty talk
The drag
Of macho brag.
Then, with heart of lead
She must to bed
There to endure the joyless ride
Of mechanical cock on mechanical bride
Why? Because he must nightly
Prove his mythed virility.
For variation, there's the drunken bout
Ravings, accusations from this lout
Insults, even threats, to be borne
Last shreds of dignity are torn
As grand finale to his drunken lies
He, triumphing, has to force
Himself between her thighs.
She prays to the god Divorce.

SNAPSHOT OF A MARRIAGE:
BIRTHDAY DINNER

On my birthday
you took me to dinner
at the Holiday Inn

unhappiness burned between us
like the candle on the table
I don't remember the menu

a typical married couple
nothing left to say

coming back from the ladies' room
I saw you trying to date the waitress
holding her hand

I remember the humiliation

Years later at night
I count my griefs
Like a miser's hoard.

INSTRUCTIONS: POWER GAMES

Don't hear me when I speak
If you hear, don't listen
Be condescending
("Acting superior" implies an inferior)
When I smile at you don't smile back
Don't laugh at my jokes
Interrupt me before I've finished speaking
Implication: I say nothing worth hearing
Read the paper when I talk to you
Ignore me in company
Tell me you'd rather be
Somewhere else, with someone else
Be cold when I'm upset
Sneer at my accomplishments
Tell me I should be thinner,
Taller, smaller, blonder
Anything but what I am
Tell me I'm stupid
Don't pay attention
Don't read my poetry.

DON'T CALL ME I'LL CALL YOU

At last I've learned your lesson:
Fuck and betray
Judas kisses after the party
Dawn comes, time to go boy
Time to go to work
Cup of coffee by the bed, polite smile
A firm and smiling no (but the smile is fading):
Time to go.
Give me your number, I'll give you a call
Some time
No, not this week, too busy
Already my thoughts are elsewhere
Last night's revelry receded into nuisance
A drunken "time."
Yes, I've learned your lesson:
Kiss, fuck, flatter, betray
Dismiss.
You can go now. You've served your turn in bed.
I have at last become despicable
As hard, as fast and loose as you.
Go play, boy, play
I am as callous as you are now
A Pyrrhic victory.

TRAFFIC SIGNS

I see the sign marked YIELD
And I would fain GIVE WAY
Too often have I stopped at STOP
And I have lost the way
If one like you would ask me YIELD
I would not say you nay
Too often have I stopped at STOP
And I have lost the way.

VALENTINE'S DAY

There is no possibility
of love.
There is a possibility
For rituals, formalities
Such as:
The exchange of heart-shaped chocolates
The exchange of red paper hearts
With "FOR MY VALENTINE"
Written in fancy letters;
The eating of heart-shaped cakes
Smothered with sweet innocent icing
The icing on the cake: too much!
We eat with polite murmurs
Trifling the icing with our forks
We eat sweet things
We behave sweetly
We kiss our Valentines
We talk about our birthstones
As if someone (a lover)
Were going to shower us with jewels
We kiss formally
We display our lovers
Meanwhile knowing, my darling,
You are having an affair
With someone else.

In/nocence

When I was married
I wanted to sit on my husband's lap
Curled up like a little girl, a baby
I wanted to go to bed with a headache
And for him to bring me a cup of tea
And warm my cold feet. He did
But he always wanted to screw
He spoiled it all
How can I play the innocent ingenue
When I always have to screw?

My analyst said
I wanted him for a father, not a lover
That it was my fault he was angry
She spoiled it all
How can I play the innocent victim
As I pass through the Archway into the park
With such bitter knowledge?

The police said
It was my fault
When the strange man attacked me
Because I lived alone
They spoiled it all
They told me to get a dog
Or get my self another man
For protection.
I confess I am confused:
Who will protect me from the protector?

I no longer am
The innocent victim.
Watch out! My house is booby-trapped
With man-eating plants
There are blunt instruments
Hidden in closets and under the bed
That lamp is a disguised murder weapon
My sharpened knives are ready in the kitchen
A killer cat sits on my shoulder
Medea's drugs and potions lurk in my cabinet.

When I wake at night
My hands are stained with blood.

THIS LITTLE GIRL: AN AUTOBIOGRAPHY, BEFORE AGE 9

A little girl had freckles, pale skin
Mousey-blonde hair parted on one side
Held back from her face with plastic clips.

A little girl went out to play
They called her in and pulled her pants down
Daddy whipped her with a sjambok for disobedience.

A little girl ate elephant grass in the park
Sweet and sharp in the mouth; she swung on swings
Little girl was happy, the sun shone.

A little girl played pooh-sticks in the gutter
Made mud pies, climbed trees, stole
Luscious grapes from next-door neighbour.

A little girl went to boarding-school
The nuns gave coloured pictures of saints and Virgin
With crinkled golden edges: treasures.

A little girl learnt to masturbate from another girl
She practised it with her friend; lost innocence;
They felt like fallen women, age seven.

A little girl in bed with chickenpox
Her friend caught a fly, pulled its wings off
A little girl, jealous, squashed the fly.

A little girl was on a farm
She saw a pig being slaughtered
It screamed as they cut its throat; the blood.

A little girl swung over the stream
On dangling willow-branches
She fell in, wet her clothes, she cried.

A little girl spent her pocket-money on
Skipping-ropes made of licorice, bull's eyes
That change colour in your mouth, oh bliss.

A little girl plaited chairs from long grasses
Thunder was angels moving furniture in heaven
Rain-and-sunshine was monkeys' wedding.

A little girl at the swimming-pool, couldn't swim
Two older girls pulled her in, she
Plunged down then up, water rushed past her ears.

A little girl was rowed in a boat by her father
A green water-snake rippled through the water
A snake fell from a wild plum-tree across her daddy's shoulder.

A little girl had a cat called Robin
Who kissed her awake each morning with pink tongue
She was later destroyed for having too many kittens.

A little girl was shown how milk came from the breast
By a black woman with a piccaninni on her back
A white jet of milk arc-ing to the dust.

A little girl had dolls with curly golden hair
And knitted dresses. Black children had
Corn cobs dressed in rags. She like theirs better.

A little girl's dress was made by her mother
Cotton print, tiny blue flowers, short puffy sleeves
White cotton socks, shoes with straps and buttons.

A little girl was put to bed by her mother
"Tell me a story, tell me a story," she cried
"I don't know any stories," her mother replied.

MIDDLE AGE:
THE CLIMACTERIC

I dream of younger lovers
But don't have any, of any age
Changes in menstruation
At first a spot of blood
And then a flood
Stained sheets
Overweight
Have to buy Giantess panty-hose
One-size no longer fits
Varicose veins
I feel a lump on my breast
In the prime of life: overripe
A bruised pear with brown spots
About to rot rot rot rot....

PHOTOGRAPH

Can you photograph pain?

This is supposed to be a photograph of me:
Blubber sweat and tears
Taken at an awkward moment
I wasn't ready for it: a "candid."

You carefully compose the façade:
>   Two eyes, indifferent red
>   Two cheeks, bleached of colour
>   Cracked lips.
Below the surface   LIES
Acid eats away the face
To bare bones
The structure of the thing, sans nerves
Expressionless
"Very you, my dear!"
The perfect shot.

OR   you could do it in the negative
Simply wipe out "her best features"
Leave a blur, a black, blank
Very "expressionist"!
Prying posterity
Will never know what I am.
They say:
This is a photograph
Of nothing.

MARKING: A POEM FOR TWO VOICES

Professor:

Too many vague and unsupported generalisations.
Weak and illogical in argument.
Lacks content; obscure in style.
Documentation inadequate.
Consult *MLA Handbook* on punctuation of titles.
Too many careless errors: proofread.
Some good points, but....
Style needs more care: consult Strunk and White.

Student:

Bitch. You're full of shit.
If you don't raise my mark to 75
I'll shoot you.

MALEVOLE

Under the neon lighting   at meetings
the chairs in rows   the agendas   strategies
you feel his hatred   across the room
Who knows why?   just because
you are a woman?   the Other
a feminist   standing-for-something?
the colour of your skin?   your clothes?
your sexual preference?
Who knows?   who can fathom?
the hatred

Unexpected encounter: the elevator doors
open   his face   distorts
into a smile   a forced greeting
He is giving himself away   he is plotting your destruction
You are waiting for him   to go too far
You are waiting for him   to shoot himself
with the gun he prepared for you
Who is the spider   who the fly?
You are watching for   his fall
You know something   about hatred
you are not as innocent as you seem
you know it kills   the hater
not the hated

THE GREAT COMMUNICATOR

I wanted to burn holes in the paper

    with my words

Even you would have to pay attention

But you tell me you "never read poetry."

II. SEASONS

Bitter spring

Blossoms shaken by the wind

Lovers quarrelling

ELEMENTAL POEM

EAST   WEST   NORTH   SOUTH
EARTH   AIR   FIRE   WATER

We turn to the East: AIR
Blue space—breathing—the kiss of life
The wind driving sails and waves across the ocean
Impelling clouds across the sky.
Blowing away the cobwebs at Cape Spear
We take deep breaths and laugh.
Meditation on the breath
I watch your breathing as you sleep.

Otherwise:

Difficulty in breathing, the poisoned air
Tear gas, poison gas in the trenches
Coughing up one's guts
Emphysema, asthma, bronchitis
Choking, throttled, the breath stopped
The air that kills.

We turn to the South: FIRE
The singing kettle on the hearth
Cooking: the bubbling pot of beans
The barbecue that friends and neighbours share
The camp fire, sitting in a circle
Glowing coals, warmth in winter
Making love by firelight
Candles burning before the shrines
Solar energy
The fiery sunset flowing red
The stars dancing round the sky.

Otherwise:

Smoke from the death camps: Auschwitz
The burning of people
Witches burned alive in the burning-times
The mushroom cloud at Hiroshima
Bombed houses catching fire in Philadelphia
Napalm burns on screaming children
Caught in cross-fire
Fire that destroys.

We turn to the West: WATER
First element, the waters of life
The sea womb of the Mother Goddess, giving birth
To strange creatures, bearing exotic cargoes
Aphrodite rises from the foam
The waterfall tumbling over cliff
The holy well, the sacred spring
That heal our spirits
Swimming in the sunset
Immanence is light on water.

Otherwise:

The flood that destroys, the burst dam
The raging sea, sailors drowning
The Ocean Ranger gone, bodies never found
The water cannon on the protest march
Polluted lakes killing fish; mercury poison
The poisoned water that kills.

We turn to the North: EARTH
Gaea, Mother Earth, the Deep-Breasted One
The nurse of seedlings, infusing the blossoms
Forming the fruit
Digging our gardens
Manuring, tilling, sowing seeds
Until the bean hangs on the vine
Until the lettuces fan out their delicate leaves
Carrots, potatoes plump and swell
The fertile earth, abundantly feeding her children
At the last our final resting-place.

Otherwise:

The parched earth, desert, famine
The rain forests cut down
Defoliation—stripping the earth
Chemical warfare where nothing grows
The earth poisoned with PCBs
Eroded soil, the waste land
The bomb—nuclear winter
The poisoned earth.

EARTH   AIR   FIRE   WATER
Essential elements, natural sources, re-sources:
Extract, extort, exploit, rape, destroy, kill
Or reverence, worship, conserve the sacred grounds of being?

[This poem was written for A Women's Peace Celebration.
L.S.P.U. Hall, St. John's, 20 May, 1985.]

SUNDAY, LATE AUGUST IN LONDON

The year turns towards death
Trees stand like sentinels of loss
Knowing their green will go
Within a month
Victoria's love petrifies mourning
In bronze and stone
Already the grass is crunchy with dead leaves
I go to museums to look at pottery
Made by people long since dead
Dazed I sit on bench and trancelike
Gaze at blues and yellows
Walled in glass
Little cups, bowls, jugs
Once daily used
In the park the living seem to dominate
The waiting earth
Mothers smile as kids chase screaming
People with dogs pace serenely through the green
The wooden bench I sit on
Recalls the fragment of a Roman ship
In the museum
A few scraps of wood, a coin
Under the mast for luck
Life, so cocksure, mocked by death
The trees, unheeded, warn us of the end
Tourists take smiling snapshots
Dark clouds black the sky
Yellow leaves fall
I grope the mystery of life
The wind is chill
Time to walk briskly home to tea.

december

The way they put up the Christmas decorations in the
stores in November   next thing it's jingle bells jingle bells in
the supermarket   and people boasting they've done their
Christmas shopping in October I hate that   I hate xmas
shopping *period* and then people saying "I hope we have a
white Christmas" and I say I hope we have a green one   and I
have to mark exams   I just wish it was all over

and then you get the first xmas card and it's like the
first swallow in summer or the first cuckoo in spring and next
thing you're lingering by the unesco christmas cards and
saying aren't they expensive but I like that one THEN you see
the men selling christmas trees in Churchill Square   and I start
muttering to people "I'm going to get my plastic exmass tree
out of the closet" and ten to one Sandy says "We're going into
the woods to get our tree and why don't you come?" and I say
"Nah...then I'd have to buy one of those stands to put it in and
it will shed all over the carpet, criss-mess so to speak" and
then I say OK then but just for the ride and I bring my hatchet
and everyone argues over which tree to get   and then Michael
says "I'm going to order my goose for Christmas dinner—
Victorian" and then everyone has to contribute something and
one year I had to do the Mince Pies and I bought frozen puff
pastry and Sheilagh rolled it out and they were delicious And
then I remember the year I was writing a paper and I took a
taxi down to the Salt Box on Christmas Eve and did all my
Christmas shopping in one fell swoop

and then the sun shines on the fresh snow and people
say "It's beginning to look at lot like Christmas" and laugh   and
I think of inviting some people in for mulled wine and the party
invitations start arriving and sometimes I go to three parties in
one day over the Twelve Days of Christmas and then Morgy
said this year Would you like to go carol singing?   and I said
Oh I haven't done that since I was a kid, Good King Wenceslas
and the Holly and the Ivy and I said Yes

III. I MOVED ALL MY WOMEN UPSTAIRS

I MOVED ALL MY WOMEN UPSTAIRS

I moved all my women upstairs
Charlotte, Emily, Anne: the three sisters
Always together on my shelves;
Next to them Gaskell, biographer and friend.
I have my Sappho, my Sévigné
Austen and Dorothy Wordsworth
George Eliot, George Sand
Elizabeth Barrett Browning, Dickinson, Rich
Woolf and Collette
Violette Leduc and stern de Beauvoir.
My lesbians: *The Well of Loneliness, Ruby Fruit Jungle*, Stein;
My feminists: our Kate, Betty Friedan;
My artists: Emily Carr, Laura Knight, Judy Chicago, Cassatt;
Those women who have touched me—*The Color Purple*—with grace.
My women look at me from untidy shelves.
They speak: "Write, my daughter, my sister:
That's all that matters."

TO CHARLOTTE BRONTË

I asked myself if I was wretched or terrified.
I was neither.

Oho, Charlotte, I would have liked to meet you
As you walked alone that frosty night
"for it was by the leading of stars only
I traced the dim path"
(The darkness was inward, you said)
"I should have quailed," you said
But you didn't
"I drew in energy," you said
"A bold thought was sent to my mind,"
AND, you said, "My mind was made strong to receive it."

You arrive alone in a foreign city
"Two moustachioed men came suddenly
from behind the pillars;
they were smoking cigars,
their dress implied pretensions
to the rank of gentlemen,
but, poor things! they were very
plebeian in soul.
They spoke with insolence,
and, fast as I walked,
they kept pace with me a long way."
Tracked by the "dreaded hunters"
The sons of Belial, the "sneering simpletons"
Whose game is hunting women.

Where did you get your courage?
I do not walk alone at night
And I am bigger than you, taller
You were mistaken for a servant
I'm mistaken for a university professor
When I carry my black briefcase as a prop.
Where did you get your great heart?
Your strong mind? Your bold thoughts?
You yearned to travel, to see everything
I board a plane, suffer from jetlag
Stay in my hotel room at night
Do not go out alone in this city
Do not get into an elevator with a strange man
I put the chain on my door
Watch other people getting shot on television.

[The quotations are from Charlotte Brontë's *Villette*.]

$ALARY DI$CRIMINATION AT MUN:
A FOUND POEM

"Unworthy" women and "female incompetents"
"below average women"
need not apply
for salary redress.
Paying "female incompetents"
the same as "male incompetents"
is not an argument on which
we wish to rely.
[Footnote 14]

$$$$$

there is not necessarily
an implication
that the administration
acted *consciously*
to establish the patterns.
The presence of
statistically significant
discrimination
against women
need not imply
that any particular
administrators
acted intentionally
to keep
the salaries of women
low
with respect to
that of men (pp. 4-5)

Comment: Yes, I clearly
        see
        these decisions are made by
        nobody

    $$$$$$

multiple regression
the regressor set
professor dummy
r^2
    $$$$$$$

809 faculty members
of whom
132 are women (p. 15)

Chorus [to the tune of *Yes, we have no bananas*]:

        Yes, we have no inequality
        We have no inequality today.

      $$$$$$

a two-tail
5%
test
criterion (p. 23)

      $$$$$$$

Faculty of *Science*:

> While there is a bonus
> of $1499
> for married men
> married women
> are not only paid
> nearly $2500 less
> than their married male peers
> but are paid nearly
> $1000 less
> than unmarried male and female peers.
> This is "the married women effect."

Chorus: Women scientists! Stay single
> If you want to hear your money jingle!
> Oh Madame Curie
> If you worked at MUN today
> What would your salary be?

> $$$$$$$$$$$$$

Faculty of *Education*:

> "The sex term
> appears
> as a
> downward
> differential
> for holders of
> the doctorate.
> The doctorate
> makes a difference
> for men
> but
> not
> for women." (p. 48)

Moral: Women! don't bust your gut
> to get that doctorut:
> it doesn't make
> a damned bit
> of difference to your take
> home pay.

> Women educators! Take no spouse
> If you want money in your house.
> Marry and you'll rue the day.
> A husband means a cut in pay.

> Women educators! As you see
> It's futile to get your Ph.D.!
> Let this be understood
> Working hard won't do no good.

> $$$$$$$$$

a bias against older women
again a bias against older women (p. 49)

Moral: Women! Don't get older!
     Dye your hair!
     Get a facelift
     Lie about your age!
     It costs to be older.

N.B.   The question of redress
     is not considered
     in this paper.

$$$$$$$$$

[Quotations from *Sex Discrimination in Faculty Salaries at Memorial University: A Decade Later*. By William E. Schrank. Department of Economics. Memorial University of Newfoundland. 1985.]

the woes of whining womanhood

in that i was sexually abused by my uncle when i was 8 years old
in that i was raped in my foster-home
in that my father beat me
in that my husband beat me
in that my husband kicked me in the belly when i was pregnant
in that i was raped as a teenager hitch-hiking home
in that i was attacked by a strange man with a knife
in that the police told me a woman should not live alone
in that i was verbally insulted on the street
in that i had an abortion
in that i had to go before a committee of men to get permission
to have an abortion
in that after the abortion i dreamt of the child
in that my marriage was unhappy
in that i am a single parent
in that i had a hysterectomy
in that i had a mastectomy
in that i got my nose fixed, and people still thought i was ugly[1]
in that my high heels hurt my feet
in that i got cancer from hair dyes
in that my husband left me for a younger woman
in that i am lonely and want a man
in that i screwed a man and it was awful
in that i turned to drink
in that i got hooked on tranquillizers
in that a man with lesser qualifications got the job
in that i am paid $1900 less than my male colleagues[2]
in that my son is a male chauvinist swine already
in that my daughter has started to shave her legs

in that i was put in prison for advocating birth control[3]
in that i was imprisoned for demanding the vote
in that i was beheaded for demanding women's rights[4]
in that i was put in prison for being a prostitute
in that i was put in a mental hospital for being a lesbian[5]
in that a policeman forced me to suck his cock in a police car
in that i was gang raped
in that i am homeless and destitute
in that the welfare is not enough to live on
in that my children are hungry
in that they took my welfare away because i had boyfriend
in that i am old and people ignore me
in that i am old and sick and no one cares

IN THAT: THIS IS THE LAST WHINE OF THE WOMEN
IN THAT: FROM NOW ON WOMEN ARE GOING TO DANCE
            IN THE STREETS
IN THAT: WOMEN ARE GOING TO TAKE BACK THE NIGHT
IN THAT: FROM NOW ON WOMEN ARE GOING TO BE
            STRONG & JOYOUS & HAPPY & RICH & FREE
IN THAT: FROM NOW ON THERE WILL BE NO MORE WOES

Notes

[1] Violette Leduc

[2] at Memorial University of Newfoundland

[3] Margaret Sanger

[4] Olympe de Gouges, decapitated November 1793

[5] See Adrienne Rich, "Compulsory Heterosexuality"

BETRAYED BY WOMEN

Betrayed by women, I too bleed monthly
My mother gave me life, then squeezed it dry
The dessicated product of her womb
Her contempt was mounting
She called me "an absolute fool"
When I was growing up ugly.
Thanks, Mom, you've made my day.

Betrayed by women, brought up all wrong
How we hated each other
How we measured each breast, each hair
With jealous eyes.
"My legs are better than hers—
Look at those thick ankles
She'll never get herself a man
My waist is just so
And my breasts are
Definitely my best feature,
But my eyelashes keep falling out
(Quick, glue on false ones)
I bite my nails to the quick
He likes me better than her—
Or does he like her better?"
With such rubbish our adolescent minds were filled
We derided our female teachers
Their fancy degrees didn't get them husbands
The only true measure of success.

Betrayed by women, older and meaner
The nasty colleague, the bitchy friend
Slander and gossip, the stab in the back
Delicately or crudely delivered:
Thanks, "girls," you've made my life a misery.

Betrayed by women, betrayed by self
Self hatred, self denial
Betrayed by can't and shouldn't and oughtn't and mustn't
Declined into nothingness
The morning valium, the evening drinky-poo
Anaesthetized to nothing, waiting for the end.
We never made it, we created nothing
Put down this epitaph on my tombstone:
"She never really lived, she didn't do anything
Forget her quickly, you who pass by this stone."

EURYDICE

I was content to be dead
Wandering among the shades
Was rather peaceful really
They didn't speak, just flitted past
Sexless and mouthless
Like a silent wobble of moths;
No decisions or deceivings
No polite smiles, no promises promises
No keeping up of appearances
Or wondering what the neighbours think.
I was startled when Orpheus appeared
Monstrously alive among the dead
Sticking out like a sore thumb
In Hades (trust *him*).
Even in death he couldn't leave me alone,
Wanted sex then and there
Want to re-possess my vacant tenement.
You can't call your soul your own
In marriage.

I was too tired to argue, didn't want to make a scene
Once he has an idea in his head
He's so persistent.
As in life, I meekly, swallowing my rebellion,
Followed him. Arise and follow me.
(Why do we do it? Getting fucked.)
I was delighted when he slipped up
Turned around to look at me
(Couldn't wait)
I glided off among the dead
Melted incognito among the grey shades
Laughed in the darkness as I heard him howl
He kicked up a devil of a fuss
Screamed and shouted, but he's had his chance.
Go, Orpheo, eff off
Let me be dead in peace, won't you?

A WOMAN

Am I too silent? Am I too loud?

Am I too friendly? Am I too proud?

Am I too pushy? Am I too shy?

Am I too open? Am I too sly?

Am I attractive? Am I too fat?

Does this colour suit me? Do you like my hat?

Am I too skinny? Should I put on weight?

Am I too early? Am I too late?

Am I too brainy? Should I act dumb?

If I invited you, would you come?

Am I too sexy? Am I too pure?

Do you really like me? Are you sure?

DREAMS

I dream of missing planes, missing trains, missing buses
Missing lovers.
I am eloping with a dark handsome young man
Yes!
We have packed our suitcases, we leave secretly at dead of night
Without telling my parents
We are running away to be (at last) alone.
We run for the bus, our feet, our hearts pound
But just as we reach it, the bus goes on.
But now I have to turn back
I have left my suitcase behind
I must go back.

Another time we got to the hotel
To the room where we would (at last!) make love
In another part of the city.
He has a black dog, and so do I
But oh! my dog is lost, I must go back for it
I must phone the dog pound—I run out—
You see, I have to find the dog.

I am back at home now
Elevator doors open, revealing disapproving parents
Just as we are joining together the hands of two severed dolls
The broken hands join together—the ring!
"It is only a betrothal," I tell them, "not really a marriage."

My lover disappears. I climb a back staircase, not really scary.

Waking, I am full of regrets.
Why didn't I forget the suitcase, the dog?
Why did I turn back when we got to the room?
I know why. I was afraid.
Even when you come to me in dreams, my soul, I turn away.
You slip in and out of my dreams, in and out of my life
In both I am impotent.
The other day you phoned to invite me to party
I was "too tired" to go.

SEX POEM

Those men who haunt me in my dreams
Rubbing themselves lasciviously against me
Like the temptations of St. Anthony
So that I wake up aroused, erotic
Surprised; and the Clitoris is erect
And she shouts "Hello-o! I'm he-ere!
You haven't got rid of me yet!
Isn't sex great? I want it!"
And the dream-man presses against me in the dawn
Rubbing his prick against the delighted Clitoris
I feel pleasure, and then shame.
The Clitoris is all for going on a tear
Going to the bars, picking up a man—
Or a woman—she doesn't care which
As long as she has her pleasure.
My Head is getting anxious and worried
She warns me in a serious voice:
"Don't do it! Take care!
You'll land yourself in some scrape
Again. I beg you
Do not do anything dishonourable.

Remember all those affairs
With married men? Disgraceful,
And, for a feminist,
Not Politically Correct."
And the Heart cries out
"What about me? What of my needs?
Which are not to be satisfied
By one-night stands.
I deserve something better
Than that. What about me?"
And the Clitoris yells
"I'm horny! I'm on fire!
How about a sexual fantasy?
Ooo-ooo-ooh, what a little moonlight can doo-ooo-ooo."
Confused, I stumble out of bed
And dash into the shower
Head, Heart and Clitoris
Are screaming contradictory messages
Simultaneously
I'm going to go crazy!
I know if I listen to Clitoris
It will lead to trouble
Yet the Head is so boring, so moral
So unexciting, proper, Politically Correct
No fun
And the Heart is so fussy
No one lives up to her high standards.

What to do?
I can be virtuous and bored (emotionally dead)
Or live dangerously lascivious
But emotionally unsatisfied.
As to the Heart, I say
"There is no perfect love, no soul-mate
So forget it!"
I'd like to forget the three of them
Bury myself in a book, so to speak
If only Clitoris would stop calling:
"Hello-o-o? Yoohooo! I'm here!
I'm alive! I'm throbbing!
What are you going to doo-ooo?
Yoo-hooo! Ooo-ooh! …Ooh!"
And the Head says
"Shut up Clitoris"
And the Clitoris says
"I'm politically correct too!"

ACKNOWLEDGEMENTS

The following poems have been published: "The World Above//The World Below" and "I Wish I Could Grow Up to Be a Hag" in *Sage Woman*; "Elemental Poem" in *Atlantis* and *Up and Doing: Canadian Women and Peace*, edited by Deborah Gorham and Janice Williamson, The Women's Press, 1989; "I Moved All My Women Upstairs" and "the woes of whining womanhood" in *(f.)Lip*; "Betrayed by Women" in *Celebrating Women: Poetry and Short Stories by and about Women*, edited by Greta Nemiroff, Fitzhenry and Whiteside, 1989; "Don't Call Me I'll Call You" in *Women and Words: Poems, December 1985*, edited by Marian White; "Dreams" in *Women's Diaries: a Quarterly Newsletter*; "Traffic Signs" in *A Woman's Almanac 1987: Voices from Newfoundland*, edited by Marian White. Roberta Buchanan's work has also appeared in *Contemporary Verse 2, Canadian Dimension, The Muse, Web, Spokeswoman* and *Tickle Ace*.

Thanks to Lillian Bouzane and Marilyn Bowering who carefully read the manuscript and made valuable suggestions; and to Cathy Murphy who typed the manuscript.